# Contents

From the Editors and Contributors of *Threads*
A *SewStylish* publication

This material was previously published by *Threads*.
See page 32 for credits. All rights reserved.
First published in this format 2014

Cover Photographers: (left) Threads Staff; (top and
bottom right) Scott Phillips; (center right) Gale Zucker

Executive Editor, Series: Shawna Mullen
Assistant Editor, Series: Timothy Stobierski
Editorial Intern: Emma Kingsley

### threads

Editor: Sarah McFarland
Executive Editor: Judith Neukam
Art Director: Rosann Berry
Special Issues Technical Editor: Carol Fresia
Associate Editor: Stephani L. Miller
Assistant Editor: Dana Finkle
Special Projects Editor: Sarah Opdahl
Senior Copy/Production Editor: Jeannine Clegg
Assistant Art Director: Gloria Melfi
Administrative Assistant: April Mohr
Seamstress: Norma Bucko

threadsmagazine.com
Executive Web Producer: Victoria North
Web Producer: Evamarie Gomez
Web Editorial Assistant: Alex Lombardi

*Taunton's SewStylish* (ISSN: 1935-8482) is published by
The Taunton Press Inc., Newtown, CT 06470-5506.
Telephone 203-426-8171

**The Taunton Press**
Inspiration for hands-on living®

The Taunton Press, Inc., 63 South Main Street, PO Box 5506,
Newtown, CT 06470-5506
e-mail: tp@taunton.com

*Threads®, Taunton's SewStylish®,* and *Taunton's CraftStylish®* are
trademarks of The Taunton Press, Inc., registered in the U.S. Patent
and Trademark Office.

The following names/manufacturers appearing in *Beaded Gifts* are
trademarks: Elmer's®, Fray Check™, Nymo®, PerfectSew®

Library of Congress Cataloging-in-Publication Data in progress

ISBN: 978-1-62710-773-0

Printed in the United States of America
10 9 8 7 6 5 4 3 2 1

| | |
|---|---|
| Create Colorful Fabric Beads | 2 |
| Knotted Fabric Buttons and Beads | 4 |
| Three's a Charm Necklace | 8 |
| Fabric-Bound Beads | 12 |
| Button Bangles | 14 |
| Get Your Bead On | 16 |
| Bead Like a Pro | 18 |
| Pleated & Beaded Scarf | 20 |
| Beading on the Edge | 24 |
| Leather Bag Impact | 26 |
| Credits | 32 |

# Create Colorful Fabric Beads

For a quick gift or fast project, craft these enchanting fabric beads with just a few simple supplies. Three wraps is all it takes: fabric, yarn, and beaded wire. Lightweight, easy to string, and colorful, the beads can quickly become part of a chunky necklace, earrings, or buttons. Whether fancy and frivolous or understated and sophisticated, the design options are endless. For this project, raveling fabrics and stray threads add to the festive effect. Just follow these easy steps.

**SHARON BENTON**—Q42DESIGNS.COM.

## Supplies

- Plastic drinking straws
- Fabric scraps
- Fabric glue
- 8- to 10-inch-long yarn (eyelash or other textured yarns) per bead
- 12-inch-long 24- or 26-gauge (thin) wire per bead
- Seed beads or other small beads

**1 PREPARE THE STRAWS AND FABRIC.** For each bead, cut the straws 1¼ inches long. Cut 3-inch by 1½-inch strips of fabric.

**2 WRAP THE BEAD.** Run a small line of glue on the straw. Place the glued straw on a short end of the fabric strip and roll. Dot glue to the opposite end of the fabric to secure the fabric roll.

**3** **LEAVE A 2-INCH-LONG END OF YARN** before and after wrapping it around the roll. Tie the two ends in a knot. Trim the ends or leave them as is.

**4** **ANCHOR THE WIRE.** Bend the wire 2 inches from one end. Place the roll in the bend and twist (in twist-tie fashion) to secure.

**5** **STRING THE BEADS ON THE LONG WIRE** tail up to 2 inches from the end. Wrap the beaded wire around the roll, and twist the tails together. Tuck or coil the tails.

# Knotted Fabric Buttons and Beads

Have a few fabric scraps lying around—little scraps you have been saving for years? Well, you were right, there is a good use for them. Almost any fabric or leather can be knotted, rolled, padded or wrapped into decorative shapes you can use in place of ordinary beads or buttons. You can string them into necklaces or stitch them, make then durable with glue or leave them with a soft finish, and embellish them all you want with additional stitches, beads, and other surface effects.

Making little fabric gems is quick and easy, and you'll find everything you need around your home: a sturdy needle, scissors, knitting needles or nails, and some white glue. Fabric beads and buttons tend to be oversized, but, depending on how you choose to pair them with other elements in your wardrobe, they can be inconspicuous, outrageous, or anything in between. The only thing they won't be is ordinary.

**DIANE ERICSON** *is a contributor to* Threads.

## Supplies

- Assortment of five- to eight-inch-long fabric strips in the fabrics of your choice
- Scissors
- Needle
- Thread
- Knitting Needle or Nail
- White glue

**tip** **CHOOSING FABRIC**

Different fabrics create different looks, the main thing you need to know about your fabric is whether you like the way it looks when it is knotted. To see how your fabric will knot, twist a length of it and tie it in an overhand knot. If you are using a thin piece of fabric and want a larger knot, you will need to wrap it around another scrap to add bulk.

## Make a basic button

This thin, flat, bowlike knot is ideal for buttons and decoration.

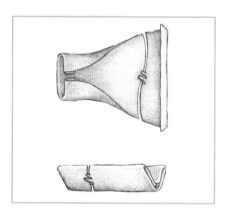

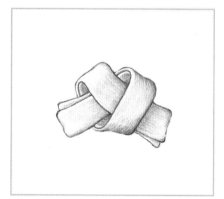

**1 START WITH A 5- TO 8-INCH-LONG STRIP.** Fold in the ends first, then fold in the sides.

**2 TIE AN OVERHAND KNOT AS SHOWN,** keeping the fabric flat. Tighten as much (or little) as you like. The tail ends are part of the design, but you can tuck one out of sight for variation.

**3 IF THE FABRIC IS SLIPPERY,** shoot a small amount of white glue into a fold or two before tightening to hold the knot in place.

# Twist, turn and glue

You don't have to use a bias strip but some fabric prints will look more interesting on the bias, and bias strips roll nicely into tubes. Knit fabrics work fine. You can leave raw edges exposed or fold them completely out of sight before making your knot. To make beads in graduating sizes, the strip you make your knot from and/or the filling materials you use to pad it with has to increase or decrease in thickness (to step the beads up or down).

## Make a Basic Bead

This sphere is ideal for beads or ball buttons.

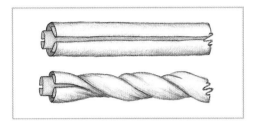

**1** UNLESS YOU WANT TO EXPOSE THE EDGES, fold a long, narrow strip as described for the overhand knot (see the drawing on the facing page), then twist the strip two or three times. Keep it twisted as you knot.

**2** START AN OVERHAND KNOT IN THE MIDDLE OF THE STRIP, but don't pull the tail through; leave a loop.

**3** SLIP THE FREE TAIL THROUGH THE LOOPED TAIL, then tighten the loop by pulling the tail.

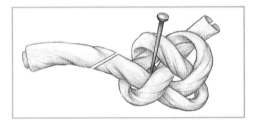

**4** MAKE AN OPENING BETWEEN THE STRANDS IN THE KNOT WITH A NAIL, trim one tail, put a drop of glue in the opening, and tuck the tail into it. Repeat for the other tail. For buttons, you can leave the tails out for sewing into a seam.

## Make a Braided Bead

This flat bun-shaped knot is ideal for buttons.

**1** TIE AN OVERHAND KNOT leaving the center open.

**2** WRAP ONE LONG END OF THE STRIP around the loop until you come halfway around. Repeat with the other end, snugging the loop until it's full and tight.

**3** TO FINISH THE ENDS, trim the tips at an angle, make a space in the strands using a nail or other sharp tool, shoot in a little glue, then tuck the end into the glue.

## Make a Rolled Bead

These work best with glue-wet fabric. Makes cylindrical beads. Works best with natural fibers and blends. If you use a bias strip, you can bend the rolled, wet tube into interesting shapes.

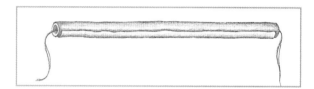

**3** **REMOVE THE NEEDLE CAREFULLY,** leaving the roll on the string to dry. Roll the tube as it dries to help keep it round.

**1** **CUT AND WET A RECTANGLE OF FABRIC** (an 8- by 2-inch piece yields 8 beads). Squeeze out excess liquid.

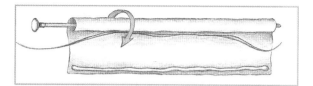

**2** **LAY THE FABRIC FLAT** on a smooth work surface (covered if necessary with waxed paper), and roll it over a knitting needle and a strong string (nylon upholstery thread works well). When you reach the edge, run a line of glue along the edge, then roll the tube back and forth several times to smooth.

**4** **SLIDE TUBE OFF THE STRING WHEN DRY,** and cut with heavy scissors into beads. Dip strung beads in polyurethane, hang, and spread out to dry on the string.

## Make a Toggle Bead

These work well in leather or kimono and tapestry fabrics.

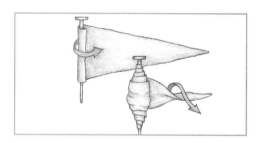

**1** **START WITH A TRIANGLE OF TAPESTRY FABRIC.** The triangle's base width is the length of the bead. The height determines the bead thickness.

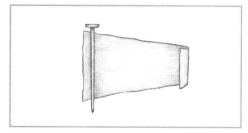

**2** **WET YOUR FABRIC,** or if using dry material, just add glue to the ends. Roll around a nail or needle. To add thickness and texture, twist fabric near the end as you wrap. Tuck the tip under one of the folds, adding an extra dot of glue.

**3** **FOR A FLATTER SHAPE,** cut off the pointed end of the triangle. The end can be smoothed down with glue, turned under, and glued or sewn down with decorative stitches or beads.

# Finishing

After knotting, trim the ends and tuck them out of sight with a needle or nail. If you have added filling, remove it entirely so the ends will be as thin as possible. You can stitch the tail ends or hold the in place with a spot of glue. Put a drop of glue on the tail, then tuck it into the bead. For a waterproof finish, string your creations on heavy thread and dip the strand into clear glossy- or satin-finish polyurethane and hang the strand to dry.

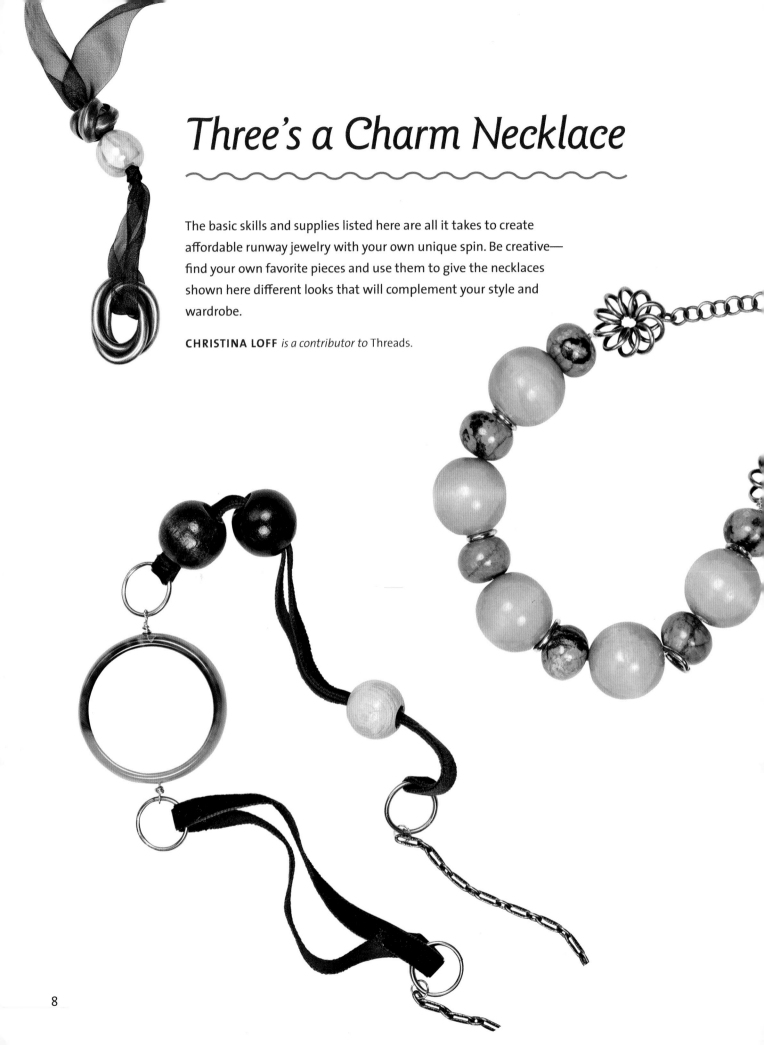

# Three's a Charm Necklace

The basic skills and supplies listed here are all it takes to create affordable runway jewelry with your own unique spin. Be creative—find your own favorite pieces and use them to give the necklaces shown here different looks that will complement your style and wardrobe.

**CHRISTINA LOFF** *is a contributor to* Threads.

# Adjustable ribbon necklace

This adjustable ribbon necklace reminds us that summer is just around the corner. Mix bright colors with chunky beads and brass, and let everyone know you aren't afraid to say what's on your mind.

## Supplies

- Two, 4-inch-long pieces of chain
- 28 inches of ribbon
- 6 round turquoise beads
- 5 large round yellow wooden beads
- 2 brass spiral flowers
- 7 large jump rings
- 15 inches of 16- or 18-gauge wire
- Flat-nose pliers
- Wire cutters
- Round-nose pliers

**1** LOOP THE RIBBON THROUGH THE LAST LINK IN ONE 4-inch-long piece of brass chain. Attach the other end of the chain to the brass spiral flower. If you can't open a link in the chain with flat-nose pliers, attach a jump ring to the chain, connect it to the spiral flower, and close it with flat-nose pliers.

**2** INSERT ONE END OF THE WIRE INTO THE OPPOSITE SIDE OF the spiral flower. Make a loop, leaving 1 inch of wire hanging down. To secure the wire to the flower, wrap the 1-inch-long end of the wire around the loop twice. Using the wire cutters, clip off the excess short wire.

**3** ALTERNATING ONE TURQUOISE BEAD, ONE yellow wooden bead, and one large jump ring, string the wire. Once you have six turquoise beads, six yellow beads, and five jump rings on the wire, connect it to the other brass flower by making a wrapped loop, as you did in step 1.

**4** COMPLETE THE NECKLACE. ATTACH THE OTHER 4-inch-long chain to the second spiral flower as you did in step 2.

**5** LOOP THE RIBBON THROUGH THE END LINKS IN THE BRASS chain. To adjust the length of the necklace, pull the ribbon. After you've determined the desired length, tie a bow, which will act as a clasp.

# Finders Keepers necklace

This simple ribbon necklace is great for showcasing odd or inspiring pieces. Look for the perfect eye-grabbing piece at your local bead shops, garage sales, or flea markets.

## Supplies

- 34 inches of sheer black ribbon
- 2 or 3 bold brass pieces
- 1 glass bead
- 1 metal ring
- 1 brass clasp
- Scissors

**1 STRING THE RIBBON.** Insert the ribbon through the object that will be the pendant (here, a brass piece). Bring the ends of the ribbon together to center the pendant.

**2 MAKE SEVERAL KNOTS ABOUT 1 INCH ABOVE THE PENDANT.** Keep the ends of the ribbon even as you do this. The pendant should now be hanging on a loop beneath the knots, as shown at left.

**3 STRING THE GLASS BEAD.** String both ends of the ribbon through the glass bead.

**4 STRING THE SECOND BRASS PIECE.** String both ends of the ribbon through it so it falls directly on top of the glass bead. Separate the ribbon ends.

**5 TIE ONE END OF THE RIBBON TO THE METAL RING.** Make several secure knots in the same place, then cut off the excess ribbon.

**6 TIE THE OTHER END OF THE RIBBON TO THE BRASS CLASP.** Make several secure knots in the same place; then cut off the excess ribbon.

# Add It Up! necklace

The way these wooden beads move on the velvet ribbon is reminiscent of an abacus, making this the perfect gift for any number-lover in your life.

## Supplies

- 18 inches of thick brass chain
- 28 inches of velvet ribbon
- 3 oversize wooden beads
- 1 large agate or glass ring
- 4 oversize jump rings
- 2 head pins, or wire if your large ring does not have holes for head pins
- Needle
- Thread to match the color of your ribbon
- Flat-nose pliers
- Round-nose pliers
- Wire cutters
- Scissors

**1 INSERT A HEAD PIN INTO THE AGATE RING.** Insert the pin through one of the holes in the agate ring from the inside to the outside of the ring. If your ring does not have holes on either side for head pins, wrap wire around each side of the ring, and create a closed loop that you can use to connect the jump rings.

**2 CREATE A LOOP WITH THE EXCESS WIRE FROM THE HEAD PIN:** Using flat-nose pliers, bend the wire toward you in a 90-degree angle. Then, using the round-nose pliers, slowly wrap the wire away from you and over the tip of the pliers until it forms a closed loop. Cut off the excess wire with the wire cutters.

**3 ATTACH ONE OF THE OVERSIZE JUMP** rings to the loop. Repeat steps 1 through 3 on the other side of the agate ring.

**4 CUT 12 INCHES OF RIBBON.** Loop it through one of the jump rings attached to the agate ring. Pull the ribbon to even the ends; they should be 6 inches long.

**5 FOLD THE RIBBON ENDS BACK.** Secure with a few stitches.

**6 LOOP THE 16-INCH-LONG RIBBON THROUGH THE JUMP RING ON THE** agate ring. Fold the ribbon back onto itself and secure with a few stitches. Pull the ends even to string the three large wooden beads onto the ribbon.

**7 FINALLY, OPEN AND ATTACH JUMP RINGS TO EITHER END OF THE BRASS** chain. While the rings are open, slip one ribbon end into one jump ring and the other ribbon end into the other jump ring.

# Fabric-Bound Beads

If you've ever longed to be a jewelry designer, here's your chance. Knotting beads into a tube of fabric couldn't be easier, and the results are magnificent.

**ANNA MAZUR** *is a contributor to* Threads.

## Supplies

- Beads
- Measuring tape
- Nail polish and paint
- Fabric and Fray Check™
- Scissors
- Sewing machine and thread
- Knotting pliers
- Clasp, eyepins, endcap
- Wire-cutters
- Round-nose pliers
- Medallion (optional)

# Stuff and knot

Wrap a measuring tape around your largest bead to figure out the width of your tube. All beads should be about the same size so that they fill out the tube properly.

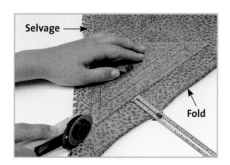

**1 CUT A BIAS STRIP.** To find true bias, fold your fabric 45 degrees to the selvage (the tightly woven edge). Cut a strip along the fold to fit the bead width, plus an ⅛-inch seam allowance). To allow for knotting, make sure that the strip length is three times the finished length of the necklace. Piece the strip as necessary to get that length.

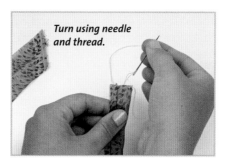

**2 SEW A TUBE.** With right sides together, machine-sew the tube using an ⅛-inch seam allowance. Stretch the tube as you sew. Turn it right-side out using a needle and doubled thread.
*TIP: Set your stitch length to 15 stitches per inch so that the stitches don't pop when you stuff the beads.*

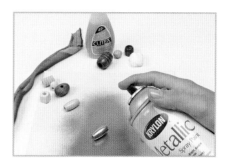

**3 PAINT WOODEN BEADS.** Give wooden beads metallic shine. In a well-ventilated area, wipe the beads with nail polish remover to remove existing varnish, and then spray paint them. Let them dry completely.

**4 ADD A MEDALLION (OPTIONAL).** If you want to add a center medallion, add it before you stuff the tube with beads. Double the tube as shown, and then slip it through the medallion. Push the two raw tube ends through the loop to secure.

**5 STUFF AND KNOT.** If you aren't using a medallion, knot one raw end of the tube. Insert a bead. Tie a knot using knotting pliers to get a tight, flush fit. Repeat for the length of the necklace.
*TIP: Use glass and plastic beads to give the necklace sparkle.*

# Add a clasp

On a long, slip-over-your-head necklace simply knot the ends. For a choker style, you'll need to add a clasp.

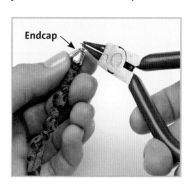

**6 ATTACH AN ENDCAP.** Insert an eyepin over the last knot. Add an endcap. With round-nose pliers, form a partial loop.

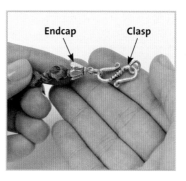

**7 INSERT THE CLASP.** Attach the decorative clasp to the endcap's partial loop, and then close the loop. Repeat this process at the other end of the necklace.

# Button Bangles

Do you love buttons? Do you collect them madly and impulsively? If so, you'll enjoy showing them off with these attention-grabbing bracelets. You will need lots of buttons—about 150. (If you don't have enough, here's a perfect excuse to buy more.)

You can make a bracelet that's elegant, funky, or subtle, depending on the buttons you choose and the way you combine them. There's a bracelet for just about every taste, so they make fantastic gifts. It's all about finding the right combination to suit the lucky friend for whom you're making it.

Once you've gathered a pile of buttons you like, it's time to arrange them into a button work of art.

**MARLENE O'TOUSA** *is a contributor to* Threads.

## Supplies

**FOR SAFETY PIN BUTTON BANGLE**
- Black elastic cord
- Small safety pins
- Spray paint (optional)
- Shank buttons

**FOR GLASS BUTTON BANGLE**
- White or clear elastic cord
- Round glass buttons
- Permanent markers

**FOR RIBBON CUFF**
- Large shank buttons
- 1- or 1½ inch-wide ribbon
- Small button for closure
- ¼-inch-wide ribbon loop

## Safety pin button bangle

Small safety pins create a dainty accessory. Larger pins mean a larger cuff. To give either style more presence, attach more safety pins to the original ones.

**1 CHECK THE FIT.** Wrap elastic cord around your wrist, leaving an extra inch at each end (for tying later). The fit should be snug but not tight. *TIP: To prevent the ends of the cord from fraying, seal them with a drop of Elmer's® glue.*

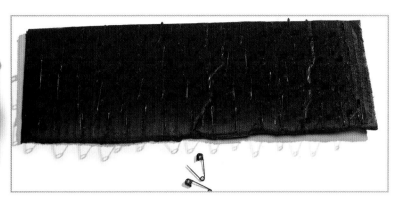
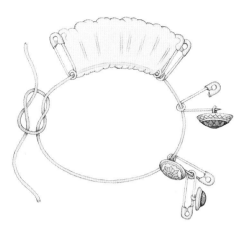

**2** **SPRAY-PAINT THE SAFETY PINS.** (Any color you want!) Stick the pins into a piece of cardboard. Then spray them from the top and all sides. Let them dry thoroughly before you remove them.

**3** **STRING ON ELASTIC CORD.** Tape one cord end to your work surface. String safety pins on the cord. Tie a square knot as shown. Then slide the buttons onto the safety pins. Build a thicker bracelet by adding more than one button to each pin. Trim the cord ends.

# Glass button bangle

Round buttons offer the look of dramatic, expensive beads but are much more affordable. For a dressy holiday accessory, combine a couple of colors as shown in the glass button bangle below.

**1** **COLOR THE CORD.** Most elastic cord comes only in black and white. To custom-color it, brush over white cord on all sides with a permanent marker. Markers come in a rainbow of colors these days.

**2** **SPACE THE BEADS.** To free up your design, vary the order of the bead colors. String on a couple of clear beads, add a purple or blue, and then add a few more clear.

# Ribbon cuff

A ribbon cuff is a great way to show off a collection of vintage buttons. Cut a wide ribbon to wrist length, plus 1 inch. Turn the ends under, and stitch them; then follow the directions below.

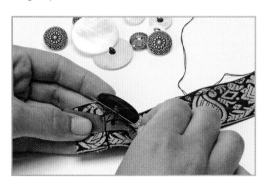

**1** **OVERLAP AND HAND SEW.** Hand-sew a small button to one end of the cuff and a corresponding loop of ¼-inch-wide ribbon to the other end. Then sew each vintage button by hand. Overlap them slightly as shown below.

# Get Your Bead On

Would you like to add some beaded glitz to a garment? Don't think twice about it. Beading is one of the easiest and most eye-catching ways to upgrade any garment—whether it's handmade or store bought. Here's what you need to know to bead a ready-made garment.

**JOANNE LEFFINGWELL** *is a contributor to* Threads.

**KNOW HOW TO HOLD IT** When beading, the fabric must be stretched and held taut. For previously constructed garments, this requires a little ingenuity since they're difficult to hoop. Holding the fabric taut with your hands may be the only option in tight places such as sleeve edges or when the garment can not be laid out any flatter, but it isn't necessarily the simplest method.

**GET READY** There are two basic methods for securing beads using needle and thread. One is to stitch down each bead individually. This is best when beads are scattered across the garment. If the thread must cross an inch or more on the underside to get from one beading spot to another, take a tiny stitch between—ideally, camouflaged next to another bead—to prevent long floats of thread.

Using a running stitch for a string of beads is faster method but is suitable only when you want a line of beading.

**KEEP DESIGN IN MIND** The weight of the beads affects the drape of the fabric and, over time, the stability of the weave. Beading must be applied so its weight is balanced on the garment. This doesn't mean counting the beads or beading only in symmetrical patterns; it means that a concentration of beads in one area should be counterbalanced. If you bead one sleeve, bead the other, too; if you bead the front of a blouse, add beads to the back as well.

**CHOOSE THE RIGHT FABRICS** You can bead on just about any fabric, as long as you prepare it. Cotton, linen, and silks work easily, but for chiffon or other lightweight fabrics, add an underlining to the beaded areas, and stitch through both layers; a second layer of the same fabric often works well. Don't work on a knit or any stretchy fabric until you're experienced with more stable fabrics and have a good sense of tension control.

Typically, it's best to match your thread color to the background fabric, but in certain instances—such as when you apply transparent beads—you should use the thread color that gives you the best overall affect. Use a single strand of thread waxed with beeswax. Wax strengthens the thread and prevents fraying and tangling.

## Supplies

- Sharps or regular beading needles
- Polyester, cotton, or silk thread that matches the fabric
- Beeswax
- Beads
- Embroidery hoop (optional)

**CARE FOR YOUR GARMENT** Garments made of washable fabric can be hand washed if the beads are colorfast. To check the colorfastness of beads, shake a few in a small jar of warm water, drain, and let dry; then compare them to their unrinsed mates. Beads that are not colorfast will be noticeably paler than those that weren't rinsed.

Most beaded garments can be cleaned by a good dry cleaner, but be careful. If a beaded garment needs ironing, either steam it without actually touching the fabric or the beads, press on the wrong side on a terry-cloth towel, or use a thick, pressing cloth. Glass beads can get hot enough to harm certain fabrics and threads.

**tip** SAVE YOUR BACK

Don't bead with your shoulders hunched up. Also, be sure to work in good lighting such as daylight when possible. Gaze outside often to give your eyes a rest.

# Get a line of shine

A simple running stitch is all that's required to add a line of beads to a garment.

**TO SEW ON THE BUGLE BEADS SHOWN ABOVE, USE A BASIC RUNNING STITCH.** Simply move the needle in and out of the fabric, pick up a bead, and then repeat.

# Types of beads used for garments

**Bugle beads**

Sizes 2 to 5 (left to right)

Silver lined

Satin

Luster

Iris

Metallic

**Two-cut beads**

Silver lined

Iris

Satin

Opaque

**Three-cut beads**

Transparent luster

Silver lined

Satin

Metallic                    Opaque

Color lined

Opaque luster

**Silver-lined rocailles**

**Seed beads**

Opaque

Transparent

Transparent iris

Luster opaque

Metallic colors

Metallic iris

Ceylon beads

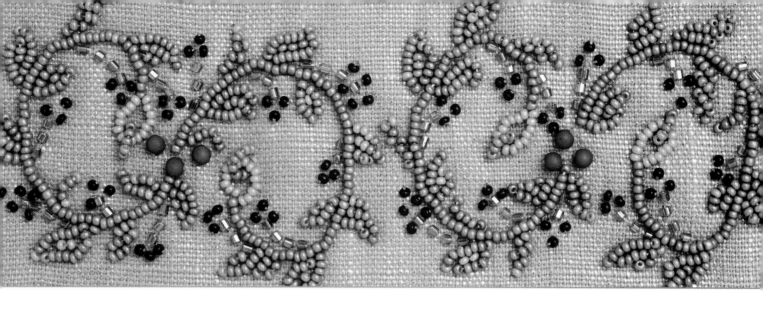

# Bead Like a Pro

Beading is a timeless embellishment that you can add to gifts of all sorts with both free-form and embroidery techniques. Here, we focus on the latter: six simple stitches that you can combine in scores of different designs.

**ANNA MAZUR** *is a contributor to* Threads.

## Supplies

- Beads
- Nymo® beading thread (All purpose/Size D)
- Sewing needle (typical beading needles are too flimsy to sew through fabric)
- Beading design and paper
- Water-soluble marking pencil
- Embroidery hoop (Optional: hoop lightweight fabric to prevent the stitches from puckering)

## 2 Basic stitches

To get started, thread your needle with one thread, and knot the end. Then bring the needle up from the wrong side of the fabric.

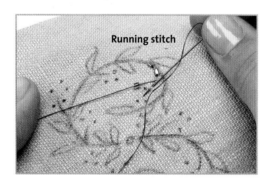

**SEW ONE BEAD AT A TIME.** Let the bead fall down the thread until it hits the fabric surface. Lay the bead on its side (with its hole parallel to the surface), and take the needle back down into the fabric a bead length away. This stitch is also known as a "running stitch."

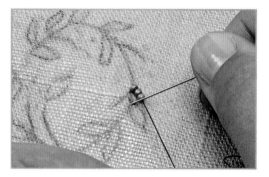

**SEW MULTIPLE BEADS.** Pick up several beads. Let the beads fall down the thread. Lay them on their sides flush against each other (with bead holes parallel to the surface), and take the needle back down into the fabric right next to the last bead.

# 4 More stitches

After you've mastered these four stitches, combine them in one design, as demonstrated at left.

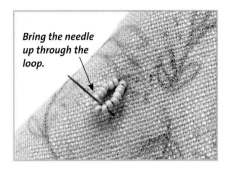

**Bring the needle up through the loop.**

## Satin Stitch

**SEW PARALLEL GROUPS OF MULTIPLE BEADS ON ONE THREAD.**
Zigzag (or "float") the thread under the fabric after each row to start the next row. The rows will butt up against each other for a "satin" look.

**TIP:** *This stitch is a variation on "Sew Multiple Beads" at left.*

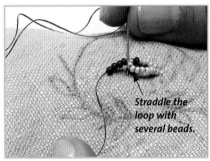

**Straddle the loop with several beads.**

## Lazy-Daisy Stitch

**PICK UP SEVERAL BEADS.** Then insert the needle back into the fabric at the same point where it came out. Pull the thread until a loop of beads forms on the right side of the fabric. Hold the loop in place, and bring the needle from the wrong side of the fabric up through the beaded loop at the loop end. Pick up enough beads to straddle the loop; then reinsert the needle through the fabric on the outside of the loop as shown above.

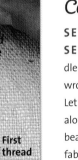

## Couching

**SEW PRE-STRUNG BEADS WITH A SECOND THREAD.** You'll need two needles. Bring up one threaded needle from the wrong side of the fabric, and string the beads. Let them fall down the thread. Lay the thread along the fabric, leaving spaces between the beads. Temporarily secure the needle in the fabric. Next, thread a second needle. Stitch over the beaded thread between every three or four beads, or as desired. Continue down the line of beads. Add more beads to the first needle as needed. To finish, insert both needles into the fabric, and knot on the fabric's wrong side.

Labels: Second thread, Second needle, First needle, First thread

## Backstitch

**HOLD DOWN SEVERAL BEADS AT ONCE.** As the name implies, the beads are sewn once and then stitched back through again. To start, bring the knotted needle up from the wrong side, and pick up four beads. Let the beads fall down the thread. Lay them on their sides flush against each other. Insert the needle back down into the fabric right next to the last bead. Bring the needle up from the underside between bead 2 and 3. Pass the needle through beads 3 and 4. Pick up four more beads, and repeat this process for the length of beads desired.

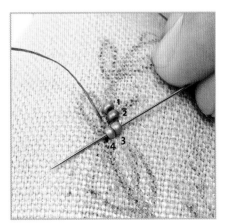

**tip**  **SECURING THE BEADS**

During the beading process, knot the thread frequently to minimize bead loss if a thread breaks within the beadwork. Simply loop and pull: Catch one or two yarns of the fabric with the needle; then pull the needle until a loop forms. Pass the needle through the loop, and pull to form a knot. To finish a thread, knot first; then cut the end close to the knot.

# Pleated & Beaded Scarf

Scarves are popular fashion accessories, available in myriad colors, fabrics, and designs. But if you're interested in setting trends rather than following them, take the time to create a unique one-of-a-kind design by adding dressed up details such as tailored tucks and hand-beading to a store-bought chiffon scarf.

Not only will your scarf stand out from the rest, you'll create an accessory that is a rich combination of color, texture, and movement. Don't be daunted by chiffon's shifty reputation; we'll teach you to tame this featherweight fabric. With just a few simple techniques, you'll be on your way to creating the perfect gift or just the scarf you need to make your own fashion statement.

**KATRINA WALKER** *is an apparel designer, sewing educator, and a contributor to* Threads.

## Prep your fabric

Chiffon is notorious for being difficult to work with, but a simple preparation of liquid stabilizer and water will keep it under control and make your sewing as smooth as silk.

Mix a little liquid stabilizer and water in a bowl. Soak the scarf, and gently knead in the mixture. Hang dry, keeping hemmed edges parallel. When dry, iron the fabric for a crisp finish.

### Supplies

- 14-inch by 72-inch silk chiffon scarf
- 70/10 universal or microtex needles
- Beading needles
- Beading thread
- Iron and ironing board
- PerfectSew® liquid stabilizer
- Seam gauge or ruler
- Sewing machine
- Silk or polyester thread
- Size 11-6 hand-washable beads

# Construct the tucks

The tucks set this scarf apart from the simple flat fabric designs available in stores. Make a series of lengthwise and widthwise tucks to form a grid pattern.

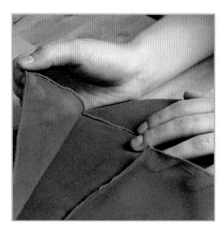

## 1 FOLD THE SCARF IN HALF LENGTHWISE.
Press along the fold to create a sharp crease.

## 2 OPEN THE SCARF, AND PLACE IT ON THE IRONING BOARD.
Fold one long edge to the center crease, and press. Repeat for the other side; keep the creases pointing toward the ironing board.

## 3 DIVIDE THE SCARF'S LENGTH IN THREE EQUAL CREASES.
Measure the difference between creases, noting the measurement. Divide the measurement by 4 to find the tuck width. For this scarf, the distance is approximately 3 inches so tucks should be ¾-inch deep. Fold the crease, and stitch the tuck distance away from the fold, holding the fabric taut while stitching. Back-tack about 3 stitches when you begin and end the stitching.

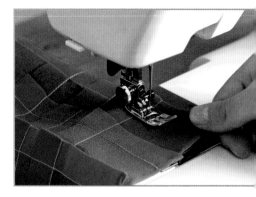

## 4 REPEAT THE PREVIOUS STEP FOR EACH CREASE.
Press the lengthwise tucks to one side.

## 5 PLACE THE SCARF WRONG SIDE UP.
Press a fold 6 inches from each scarf end as if making a hem. At each end, press two more folds the same distance apart as the lengthwise creases, moving toward the center. There should now be six horizontal creases in the scarf.

## 6 FOLD ON EACH CREASE NEAR THE ENDS OF THE SCARF TO
form the tuck. Stitch the predetermined tuck distance away from the fold, pulling the fabric taut to create tucks in a grid pattern. Press the tucks toward the scarf ends.

 YOU CAN MAKE THE SCARF, TOO

If you can't find a silk chiffon scarf you like, it's easy to make your own. Simply cut a piece of chiffon fabric to the desired size, adding a ¼ inch seam allowance, and hand-sew a tiny rolled hem along the edges.

# Dress it up with beads

Embellishing the scarf with pretty beads highlights the tuck pattern and allows you to show your creative side, and make a one-of-a-kind gift. Add a fringe of beads, a single bead—or both—to the tucks.

## Add a single drop-bead fringe

**7** **THREAD A NEEDLE WITH ABOUT 18 INCHES OF BEADING THREAD.** Tie a knot in the end of the thread. At a corner of the scarf end, unroll the hem. Insert the needle into the rolled hem so the knot will be hidden. Take a few tiny stitches toward the short end to anchor the fringe.

**8** **THREAD THE SEED BEADS AND DROP BEADS ONTO YOUR THREAD.** The last seed bead acts as a stopper. Then, insert the needle back into the drop bead and through the strung beads. Pull gently to take up the thread slack. If the strand tension is too loose, the beading thread will show. If the tension is too tight, the fringe will not hang properly.

**9** **TAKE TINY STITCHES IN THE SCARF AT THE BASE OF THE STRAND TO ANCHOR IT.** Run the needle through the hem to the next fringe spot. Take a few tiny stitches in the hem, and repeat steps 2 and 3 until you reach the other corner. Knot off at the base of the strand, hiding the thread ends in the rolled hem.

Add a bead, a fringe of beads, or both to the tuck intersections.

## Put a bead at tuck intersections

**10** **THREAD A BEADING NEEDLE WITH SILK OR POLYESTER THREAD.** Tie the ends of the thread in a knot to form a double-thread strand. Lift the tucks, and insert the needle under the tucks and through the base layer. This hides the knot. Come up through the base layer and through the tucks. Place a bead on the needle. Pass back through the layers as close as possible to the previous stitch, and repeat. Tie off the knot between layers, and bury the thread tails. Repeat for as many intersections as desired.

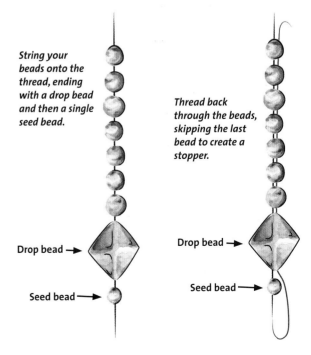

*String your beads onto the thread, ending with a drop bead and then a single seed bead.*

*Thread back through the beads, skipping the last bead to create a stopper.*

Drop bead →

Drop bead →

Seed bead →

Seed bead →

# Beading on the Edge

If you stare in awe at beaded garments and wonder how someone painstakingly placed each one of those tiny beads, keep in mind that, for many, beading is relaxing and therapeutic. We've all seen massive, extravagant patterns and designs beaded on the whole cloth, sometimes covering an entire garment and most definitely adding to the overall weight of a gown or article of clothing. You wonder how the fabric can carry the load.

But more isn't always better. Often, the best finishing touch is a subtle embellishment that catches your eye at second glance. These understated embellishments have a presence waiting to be discovered, making them even more delightful.

Take subtle embellishments placed on simple edges such as these two beaded edges for an exquisite finish. You can sew either one on a ready-made garment to infuse it with your own personal style. Or stitch them on a new garment you're making. They say, "It's all in the details," and this detail is worth considering.

**KENNETH D. KING** *is the author of* Designer Bead Embroidery. *For more information, visit CreativePub.com.*

# Create your border

These beading techniques work on almost any edge. Imagine matte silver beads on denim, clear glass beads on white organza, or jet beads on black velvet. All you need are seed beads and a beading thread as well as a needle to stitch these two edges.

## Basic Whip Stitch

This is a perfect finish for a delicate fabric: Evenly spaced spirals encircle and protect the edge. Mark the stitches on your edge; the ones shown below are ½ inch apart and ¼ inch from the edge.

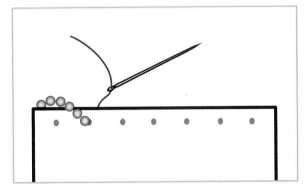

**1 SECURE YOUR THREAD BEHIND THE FIRST MARK.** Thread enough beads (fourteen or so) to reach from one dot to the next, wrapping over the edge as shown.

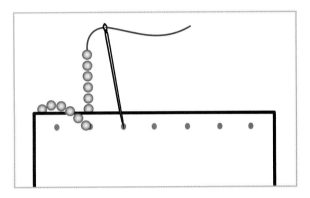

**2 INSERT THE NEEDLE INTO THE SECOND MARK FROM THE RIGHT SIDE.** Pull up the thread to complete the stitch. Repeat.

## Basic Edging Stitch

Round beads of any size will work for this edge. The beading also weights the edge.

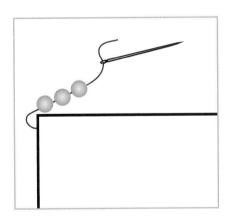

**1 SECURE THE THREAD UP THROUGH THE EDGE.** Load three beads onto your thread.

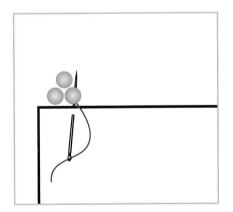

**2 ONE BEAD LENGTH AWAY, INSERT THE NEEDLE BACK** into the edge. Without passing through the fabric, insert the point through the last of the three beads, and pull the stitch tight.

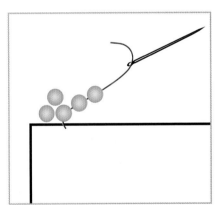

**3 LOAD TWO NEW BEADS ON THE THREAD.** As before, catch the edge of the fabric one bead length away. Again, insert the point through the last of the two beads, and pull the stitch tight. Repeat.

# Leather Bag Impact

There's nothing that beats a sumptuous leather bag or garment. Unless, it's a sumptuous leather bag or garment that's beaded with your own unique design.

**REVEREND WENDY ELLSWORTH,** *renowned seed bead artist, has traveled to Kenya to help elevate the status of Maasai and Samburu women through beadwork and education.*

## Pick your surface technique

For beading directly on leather surfaces, techniques vary according to the thickness of the leather you choose. With each method, it helps to sketch the outline of your design right onto the leather, thereby creating guidelines for sewing the beads.

**BEADING ON THIN LEATHER** If you are working with a thin leather or suede, use doubled thread that is double-knotted at the end. Pierce up through the leather with a regular beading needle. Then pick up one, two, or three beads with the needle point.

To find the natural spacing of the beads and to prevent them from buckling later, position the thread and beads flat along the surface. Then, use the last bead that was strung as a guide to push the needle back down through the suede, and pull the thread snug. If you are beading along a line, come back to the surface of the work between the last two beads, and pass the needle through the hole of the last bead to lock the beads in place. Make sure that the thread is evenly taut on the surface and underneath so the beads won't loosen. Tie off the ends of each doubled thread in a square knot on the back.

**BEADING ON THICK LEATHER** If you're beading a thick, top-grain leather such as split cowhide or elk hide, don't try to pierce through the entire thickness. Instead, make a knot, pass the needle through only the top grain (about 1 millimeter), and then pick up as many beads as you want on your needle. Carefully take a small backstitch through the top grain and then through the hole of the last bead, as shown in on the right drawing below. It is important to penetrate the full l millimeter of top grain to prevent the stitch from tearing out. If it does tear out, string another bead so you have a fresh place to stitch further down the line.

**BEAD AN EDGE** To finish a raw edge of a garment or accessory such as the edge of the flap on the purse at right, you can include touches of beaded details along the edges. To do so, thread your needle with nylon thread, pass the needle through the thickness of leather, add three or four beads, and again pass the needle through the leather close to the top edge. Bring the needle around and underneath the last bead. Then, pull tightly before you continue; repeat until the entire edge is beaded. The locking technique allows the beads to flow along the edge in a straight line.

Beading takes practice—and some time—but the unique results and the sense of pride that comes with completing a project are worth it.

# 2 Ways to bead on leather

To bead directly on the surface, choose the method that suits the weight of your leather or suede.

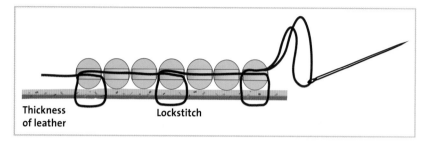

**Thickness of leather**     **Lockstitch**

**1** BEADING ALONG A LINE THROUGH THIN SUPPLE SUEDE.

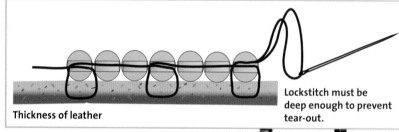

**Thickness of leather**     Lockstitch must be deep enough to prevent tear-out.

**2** BEADING ALONG A LINE THROUGH THICK TOP-GRAIN LEATHER.

### Supplies

- Beads
- Leather or suede
- Beading needles
- Beading thread

# Bead the raw edge

For little extra something, add beads to the edges of your leather pieces.

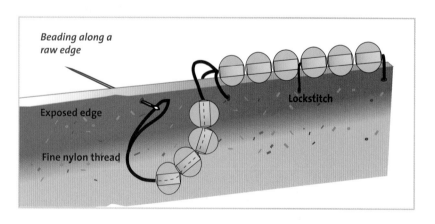

*Beading along a raw edge*

Exposed edge

Fine nylon thread

Lockstitch

# If you like this booklet, you'll love everything about *Threads*.

## Read *Threads* Magazine:

Your subscription includes six issues of *Threads* plus FREE digital access. Every issue is packed with up-to-the-minute fashions, useful techniques, and expert garment-sewing advice – all designed to help improve your skills and express your creativity.

*Subscribe today at:*
**ThreadsMagazine.com/4Sub**

## Discover our *Threads* Online Store:

It's your destination for premium resources from the editors of America's best-loved sewing magazine, designers, and sewing instructors: how-to and design books, videos, and more.

*Visit today at:*
**ThreadsMagazine.com/4More**

## Get our FREE *Threads* e-Newsletter:

Keep up with what's current – the latest styles, patterns, and fabrics, plus free tips and advice from our *Threads* editors.

*Sign up, it's free:*
**ThreadsMagazine.com/4Newsletter**

## Become a *Threads* Insider:

Join now and enjoy exclusive online benefits, including: instant videos, favorite articles, digital issues, pattern database, fun giveaways, and more.

*Discover more information online:*
**ThreadsMagazine.com/4Join**

**Look for these other *Threads* Selects booklets at www.tauntonstore.com and wherever crafts are sold.**

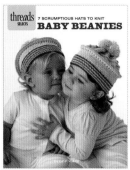

**Baby Beanies**
Debby Ware

EAN: 9781621137634
8 ½ x 10 ⅞, 32 pages
Product# 078001
$9.95 U.S., $11.95 Can.

**Fair Isle Flower Garden**
Kathleen Taylor

EAN: 9781621137702
8 ½ x 10 ⅞, 32 pages
Product# 078008
$9.95 U.S., $11.95 Can.

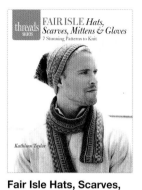

**Fair Isle Hats, Scarves, Mittens & Gloves**
Kathleen Taylor

EAN: 9781621137719
8 ½ x 10 ⅞, 32 pages
Product# 078009
$9.95 U.S., $11.95 Can.

**Prairie Girl Sewing**
Jennifer Worick

EAN: 9781621139508
8 1/2 x 10 7/8, 32 pages
Product # 078029
$9.95 U.S., $9.95 Can.

**Prairie Girl Gifts**
Jennifer Worick

EAN: 9781621139492
8 1/2 x 10 7/8, 32 pages
Product # 078030
$9.95 U.S., $9.95 Can.

**DIY Bride Cakes & Sweets**
Khris Cochran

EAN: 9781621137665
8 ½ x 10 ⅞, 32 pages
Product# 078004
$9.95 U.S., $11.95 Can.

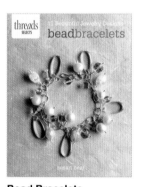

**Bead Bracelets**
Susan Beal

EAN: 9781621139515
8 1/2 x 10 7/8, 32 pages
Product # 078028
$9.95 U.S., $9.95 Can.

**Bead Necklaces**
Susan Beal

EAN: 9781621137641
8 ½ x 10 ⅞, 32 pages
Product# 078002
$9.95 U.S., $11.95 Can.

**Drop Earrings**
Susan Beal

EAN: 9781621137658
8 ½ x 10 ⅞, 32 pages
Product# 078003
$9.95 U.S., $11.95 Can.

**Small Projects to Quilt**
Joan Ford

EAN: 9781627100977
8 1/2 x 10 7/8, 32 pages
Product # 078032
$9.95 U.S., $9.95 Can.

**Cable Shawlettes**
Jean Moss

EAN: 9781621137733
8 1/2 x 10 7/8, 32 pages
Product # 078037
$9.95 U.S., $9.95 Can.

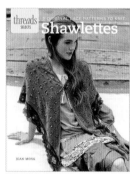

**Shawlettes**
Jean Moss

EAN: 9781621137726
8 ½ x 10 ⅞, 32 pages
Product# 078010
$9.95 U.S., $11.95 Can.

**Easy-to-Sew Flowers**
EAN: 9781621138259
8 ½ x 10 ⅞, 32 pages
Product# 078017
$9.95 U.S., $9.95 Can.

**Easy-to-Sew Gifts**
EAN: 9781621138310
8 ½ x 10 ⅞, 32 pages
Product# 078023
$9.95 U.S., $9.95 Can.

**Easy-to-Sew Handbags**
EAN: 9781621138242
8 ½ x 10 ⅞, 32 pages
Product# 078016
$9.95 U.S., $9.95 Can.

**Easy-to-Sew Kitchen**
EAN: 9781621138327
8 ½ x 10 ⅞, 32 pages
Product# 078024
$9.95 U.S., $9.95 Can.

**Easy-to-Sew Lace**
EAN: 9781621138228
8 ½ x 10 ⅞, 32 pages
Product# 078014
$9.95 U.S., $9.95 Can.

**Felted Scarves, Hats & Mittens**
Kathleen Taylor
EAN: 9781627100960
8 1/2 x 10 7/8, 32 pages
Product # 078031
$9.95 U.S., $9.95 Can.

**Easy-to-Sew Pet Projects**
EAN: 9781621138273
8 ½ x 10 ⅞, 32 pages
Product# 078018
$9.95 U.S., $9.95 Can.

**Easy-to-Sew Pillows**
EAN: 9781621138266
8 ½ x 10 ⅞, 32 pages
Product# 078019
$9.95 U.S., $9.95 Can.

**Easy-to-Sew Scarves & Belts**
EAN: 9781621138211
8 ½ x 10 ⅞, 32 pages
Product# 078013
$9.95 U.S., $9.95 Can.

**Easy-to-Sew Skirts**
EAN: 9781621138280
8 ½ x 10 ⅞, 32 pages
Product# 078020
$9.95 U.S., $9.95 Can.

**Easy-to-Sew Tote Bags**
EAN: 9781621138297
8 ½ x 10 ⅞, 32 pages
Product# 078021
$9.95 U.S., $9.95 Can.

**Easy-to-Sew Windows**
EAN: 9781621138303
8 ½ x 10 ⅞, 32 pages
Product# 078022
$9.95 U.S., $9.95 Can.

# Credits

Many of the projects, patterns, and photos in this booklet have appeared previously in issues of *Threads, SewStylish,* and/or *CraftStylish.* Listed here are the author, photographer, and *Threads* issue # or publication title.

### Create Colorful Fabric Beads
Sharon Benton. Photos: Sloan Howard. *Threads* #128

### Knotted Fabric Buttons and Beads
Diane Ericson. Photos: Sloan Howard. Illustrations: Christine Charbonneau. *Threads* #54

### Three's a Charm Necklace
Christina Loff. Photos and styling: Zach Desart and Burcu Avsar. Process photos: Sloan Howard. *CraftStylish,* Quick Stuff to Make, Summer 2008

### Fabric-Bound Beads
Anna Mazur. Photos: Scott Phillips. Process photos: Sloan Howard. *SewStylish,* Gifts to Make, Holiday 2007

### Button Bangles
Marlene O'Tousa. Detail photos: Scott Phillips. Process photos: Sloan Howard. All other photos: Judi Rutz. Illustrations: Christine Erikson. *SewStylish,* Gifts to Make, Holiday 2007

### Get Your Bead On
Joanne Leffingwell. Model photo: Jack Deutsch. Stylist: Jessica Saal. Detail photo: Sloan Howard. Charts: Joanne Leffingwell. *SewStylish,* Winter 2007

### Bead Like a Pro
Anna Mazur. Detail photos: Scott Phillips. All other photos: Sloan Howard. *SewStylish,* Gifts to Make, Holiday 2007

### Pleated & Beaded Scarf
Katrina Walker. Model photos: Gale Zucker. Stylist: Dan Pasky. All other photos: Sloan Howard. *CraftStylish,* Gifts to Make, Vol. 2

### Beading on the Edge
Kenneth D. King. Photos: Sloan Howard. Illustrations: David Rohm. *Threads* #135

### Leather Bag Impact
Reverend Wendy Ellsworth. Photos: Threads Staff. Illustrations: David Rohm. *SewStylish,* Winter 2007